WE THE PEOPLE

The
Civil Rights Act of 1964

by Jason Skog

Content Adviser: Melodie Andrews, Ph.D.,
Associate Professor of American History,
Minnesota State University, Mankato

Reading Adviser: Rosemary G. Palmer, Ph.D.,
Department of Literacy, College of Education,
Boise State University

Compass Point Books ✦ Minneapolis, Minnesota

Compass Point Books
3109 West 50th Street, #115
Minneapolis, MN 55410

Visit Compass Point Books on the Internet at *www.compasspointbooks.com*
or e-mail your request to *custserv@compasspointbooks.com*

On the cover: Demonstrators paraded from the Washington Monument to the Lincoln Memorial during the 1963 March on Washington.

Photographs ©: Bettmann/Corbis, cover, 9, 21, 25, 38; Prints Old & Rare, back cover (far left); Library of Congress, back cover, 4, 13, 14, 16, 17, 19, 22, 23, 26; New York Times Co./Getty Images, 5; Gordon Parks/Time Life Pictures/Getty Images, 7; The Granger Collection, New York, 10; Donald Uhrbrock/Time Life Pictures/Getty Images, 12; Don Cravens/Time Life Pictures/Getty Images, 15; Paul Schutzer/Time Life Pictures/Getty Images, 20; Robert W. Kelley/Time Life Pictures/Getty Images, 27; Francis Miller/Time Life Pictures/Getty Images, 28; LBJ Library photo by Cecil Stoughton, 31, 34; LBJ Library photo by Yoichi R. Okamoto, 32; Our Documents/National Archives and Records Administration, 36, 41; Joseph Louw/Time Life Pictures/Getty Images, 40.

Editor: Sue Vander Hook
Page Production: Blue Tricycle, Bobbie Nuytten
Photo Researcher: Svetlana Zhurkin
Cartographer: XNR Productions, Inc.
Library Consultant: Kathleen Baxter

Creative Director: Keith Griffin
Editorial Director: Carol Jones
Managing Editor: Catherine Neitge

Library of Congress Cataloging-in-Publication Data
Skog, Jason
 The Civil Rights Act of 1964 / by Jason Skog
   p. cm.—(We the people)
Includes bibliographical references and index.
 ISBN-13: 978-0-7565-2459-3 (library binding)
 ISBN-10: 0-7565-2459-8 (library binding)
 ISBN-13: 978-0-7565-3211-6 (paperback)
 ISBN-10: 0-7565-3211-6 (paperback)
1. United States. Civil Rights Act of 1964—Juvenile literature. 2. Civil rights—United States—History—20th century—Juvenile literature. I. Title. II. Series.
KF4744.5151964.S58 2007
342.7308'5—dc22   2006027087

TABLE OF CONTENTS

FREE BUT NOT EQUAL

Before 1964, African-Americans didn't have equal rights in the United States. In the South, there were signs everywhere that ordered them to be segregated, or separated, from white people: Colored Drinking Fountain, White Ladies Only, Exclusive Colored Theater, For Use By White Persons, No Negroes Allowed.

Blacks had to use their own drinking fountain in front of the county courthouse in Halifax, North Carolina, in 1938.

4

Blacks had to enter a movie theater through their own entrance and sit in a section separate from whites.

African-Americans weren't allowed to eat next to white people in restaurants. They couldn't sit with white people on buses or enjoy a movie from the same part of a theater. Black people had separate drinking fountains and public bathrooms. Many businesses didn't hire black employees, and local laws made it difficult for blacks to vote.

Those who didn't obey the signs were kicked out of businesses, arrested, or beaten. Some were killed. Segregation was worse for schoolchildren. Black students had to attend their own schools; they weren't allowed to go to schools where whites attended. Many black schools were run-down, one-room shacks that were either terribly hot or uncomfortably cold. Small wood stoves heated the schools in the winter. States didn't spend much money on education for blacks. Some states spent 10 times more on white students than they did on blacks.

The signs—and the ugly racism that went with them—had been around since the Civil War ended in 1865. They were a common sight in the 11 Southern states that had

*A poorly furnished grade school classroom at an African-American
school in 1956*

withdrawn from the United States in 1861 and formed the Confederate States of America. For years, the people in those states fought to keep slavery legal.

Although Abraham Lincoln's Emancipation Proclamation officially banned slavery in the South on January 1, 1863, former slaves and their children and grand-children were far from free. After the Civil War, the federal government passed the Civil Rights Act of 1866. It stated that all persons born in the United States were citizens—it didn't matter what race they were. The 13th, 14th, and 15th Amendments to the U.S. Constitution were also passed to protect the rights of freed slaves.

However, in the 1890s, Southern states and some nearby Northern states began adopting what were called black codes. These laws made it illegal for African-Americans to go into many stores and restaurants. At some restaurants, blacks could order food to go, but they had to enter through a back door to pick it up. Most public rest-rooms and drinking fountains had separate facilities for blacks and whites. Many Northern states practiced black codes without making them into formal laws.

Later, in the 1900s, African-Americans would have to pay more than whites to see a movie. The balcony would be the only place they could sit. The laws also controlled what kind of work African-Americans could do, where they could meet, and how they could talk to white people.

Black codes were called Jim Crow laws. The name "Jim Crow" was first heard in 1832 when comedian Thomas "Daddy" Rice performed the song "Jump Jim Crow" on a New York stage. Rice, who was white, wore blackface, a dark makeup that made him appear to be African-American. His acting and singing made fun of African-

Thomas "Daddy" Rice performed as Jim Crow.

9

JIM CROW.

NEW YORK.

Published by Firth & Hall, No 1 Franklin Sq

*A highly stereotypical song sheet featured Thomas "Daddy" Rice
in his racist blackface performance.*

Americans and what he called their "comic" lifestyle.

Before long, the name Jim Crow was used as a racial slur to refer to African-Americans. Laws restricting what blacks could do were thus called Jim Crow laws.

For more than 100 years, African-Americans had been looked down on and forced to live in poor conditions. In 1964, the United States would begin moving away from racial segregation toward integration. Blacks and whites would be able to live in the same neighborhood, eat at the same restaurants, go to the same schools, vote together, and sit where they wanted on a bus.

But getting to that point was often a violent struggle. Thousands of people were arrested, hundreds were hurt, and many were killed. The issue divided the nation, broke up friendships, and split communities. In the end, the Civil Rights Act of 1964 would give all citizens the same rights—regardless of skin color, religious belief, or gender. It made Jim Crow laws illegal and changed America forever.

DEFYING THE LAW

In the 1950s and 1960s, blacks and some whites worked hard to end racial discrimination. They especially wanted to end the Jim Crow laws. Their struggle for equality led to hundreds of demonstrations, protests, and quarrels.

African-Americans some-times protested by marching through the streets holding signs that condemned inequality. Other times, they gathered to pray. A number of them, such as members of the Black Panthers, used more forceful ways to demand civil rights. Some refused to follow Jim Crow laws, and many decided to

Demonstrators picketed in 1960.

12

disobey the ugly signs—they refused to sit in the back of a bus or give up their seats for whites as the law required.

They walked into restaurants reserved for whites and ordered food. In restaurants where they were allowed, some defied signs directing blacks to sit in the back and, instead, sat where they pleased. As a result, they were beaten and

A group of African-Americans tried to be served at a lunch counter in Nashville, Tennessee.

arrested. Others tried to go to white colleges where class-
mates shouted insults and threatened them with violence.

In 1955, in Montgomery, Alabama, a black seamstress
named Rosa Parks was arrested for disobeying one of the
Jim Crow laws. After refusing to give up her seat on a bus
to a white man, she was fingerprinted and jailed. Blacks

*Rosa Parks was arrested and fingerprinted for refusing to move to the
back of a Montgomery, Alabama, bus in 1955.*

in Montgomery protested by refusing to ride city buses for more than a year. Eventually, their boycott would pay off.

One of the main leaders of the bus boycott was the Reverend Martin Luther King Jr. Two years before the boycott, 24-year-old King had become the pastor of the Dexter Avenue Baptist Church in Montgomery. He began preaching and speaking against racial discrimination, hatred, and violence against blacks. He also began the Southern

Martin Luther King Jr. shared his bus boycott strategies with (seated, left to right) the Reverend Ralph Abernathy, Rosa Parks, and other black leaders.

15

People marched for equal rights, integrated schools, and decent housing.

Christian Leadership Conference, a group of church leaders
who began to rally for equal rights.

Ministers, along with thousands of their church members and other citizens, began protesting, sometimes in

16

silent marches along streets, carrying signs that objected to racial prejudice. Blacks and whites alike were fighting for equal rights for African-Americans.

A 1963 civil rights demonstration in Birmingham, Alabama, began with prayers.

Many people organized protests, demonstrations, and marches that usually were peaceful. Other times, protesters gathered to hold candles, sing, and pray. It was part of what came to be known as the civil rights movement, which helped pave the way for the passage of the Civil Rights Act of 1964.

17

PEACEFUL PROTESTS, VIOLENT OUTCOMES

Peaceful protests against racial segregation didn't always end peacefully. What usually began with prayer, singing, and marching often ended with police officers in riot gear swinging clubs and arresting demonstrators. The efforts of the protesters would eventually bring about change.

One protest was held after a 1960 decision by the U.S. Supreme Court. The court ruled that blacks didn't have to sit in separate sections of trains, buses, planes, and other public transportation that crossed state borders.

To test the new ruling, groups of blacks and whites boarded buses, trains, and planes, and traveled throughout the South on what were called Freedom Rides. Even though what they were doing was legal, Freedom Riders were attacked by mobs like the Ku Klux Klan, whose members hated anyone who wasn't white. Some buses were attacked with firebombs, or containers full of fuel that

Members of the Freedom Riders watched as their bus burned in 1961.

would explode and catch fire on impact.

For six months, more than 1,000 people participated in Freedom Rides. Violence against them was so brutal that President John F. Kennedy sent 50 federal marshals to protect them. People around the world heard about these protesters on the news. They were becoming aware of how serious racial discrimination was.

In 1963, in Birmingham, Alabama, police officers tried to get rid of a group of black protesters. They released attack

Freedom Riders Julia Aaron, David Dennis, and 25 others were protected by National Guardsmen on their bus ride from Montgomery, Alabama, to Jackson, Mississippi.

dogs on the group. Firefighters sprayed the demonstrators—
some of them children—with fire hoses so powerful that
the force of the water could peel bark off trees. Public safety
commissioner T. Eugene "Bull" Connor was in charge.
When an injured protester had to go to the hospital, Connor
smiled and said, "I'm sorry I missed it. I wish they'd carried
him away in a hearse."

*Firefighters sprayed black demonstrators with fire hoses during a protest
against segregation in Birmingham, Alabama, on May 7, 1963.*

At a protest on April 12, Connor arrested Martin Luther King Jr. for protesting without a permit. From jail, King wrote what later became a book titled *Letter from Birmingham Jail*. He wrote that disobeying the law, or civil disobedience, was right in the face of unfair laws.

T. Eugene "Bull" Connor opposed integration.

National news programs televised some of the demonstrations that occurred after King's arrest. Police officers clashing with protesters shocked the public as well as the president of the United States.

With violent attacks on African-Americans increasing, people were not safe in their homes. On June 12, a

People gathered at a memorial service for Medgar Evers following his murder in 1963.

civil rights leader named Medgar Evers got out of his car
at his Jackson, Mississippi, home. He was field secretary for
the National Association for the Advancement of Colored
People (NAACP), one of the nation's most respected civil
rights organizations.

In his hand was a stack of T-shirts that stated "Jim
Crow Must Go." As he walked to the door, he was shot
and killed.

PRESIDENT KENNEDY'S PROMISE

Shortly after he was elected in 1960, President John F. Kennedy introduced a civil rights bill. When it went to Congress for approval, however, it was quickly and quietly ignored.

After the violence and trouble in Birmingham in 1963, Kennedy decided to act. He sent National Guard troops to the outskirts of Birmingham, hoping to calm the growing anger on both sides. It helped, and a group of white business owners agreed to integrate their stores and lunch counters. They allowed black customers to eat and shop with whites. But that didn't end discrimination.

Tensions continued to grow in the segregated South, and Kennedy was concerned. On June 11, 1963, he addressed the nation in a televised speech. He told people about a new, broader civil rights bill that he wanted Congress to consider.

"The fires of frustration and discord [conflict] are

President Kennedy spoke to the nation about civil rights on June 11, 1963.

burning in every city," Kennedy said. He told television viewers how protests were creating tension and added, "We face, therefore, a moral crisis as a country and as a people." The president asked Congress to pass a law that would give all Americans equal rights. All people, he believed, deserved to go to public places—hotels, restaurants, theaters, retail stores, and other establishments. "Its denial is an … indignity that no American in 1963 should have to endure," he stressed.

Civil rights leaders set out to help Kennedy's bill get passed. They organized a march in Washington, D.C., the nation's capital, to encourage Americans to support the bill.

Organizers had hoped that 100,000 marchers would show up. But on August 28, 1963, more than 250,000 people—including 60,000 white people—arrived in

The Reverend Martin Luther King Jr. encouraged his audience in Washington, D.C., to remember that all men are created equal.

26

Washington, D.C. Thirty trains, 2,000 buses, and countless cars had carried them there. Blacks, whites, young, and old came from all over the country and marched side by side.

A massive crowd gathered in Washington, D.C., at the March on Washington for Jobs and Freedom on August 28, 1963.

It was the largest demonstration for human rights the country had ever seen.

At the end of the rally, King stood in front of the Lincoln Memorial and spoke to the huge crowd. "I have

King addressed the crowd at the Lincoln Memorial in Washington, D.C.

The March on Washington and the Freedom Rides helped make citizens throughout the country aware that the civil rights of African-Americans were not protected.

a dream," he said, "that my four little children will one day live in a nation where they will not be judged by the color of their skin but by the content of their character."

His speech energized the crowd and came to symbolize the struggle for racial equality.

The march made many Americans aware of racial prejudice and segregation in their country. But most racists, like those in Birmingham, were not moved after seeing the march. Some responded with more violence. About two weeks after the march, a black church in Birmingham was bombed; four school-age girls were killed. The church had been a center for civil rights meetings. That same day, a 13-year-old black teenager riding on the handlebars of his brother's bicycle was fatally shot by a group of white teens.

Three months after the march, tragedy struck the entire nation. On November 22, 1963, President Kennedy was shot and killed in Dallas, Texas. Vice President Lyndon B. Johnson took over as president. Immediately he vowed to carry on Kennedy's hope for equal rights. On November 27, in his first address as president, Johnson urged the passage of the civil rights bill.

Lyndon B. Johnson was sworn in as president aboard the presidential jet, Air Force One. *On his left was Jacqueline Kennedy, former first lady of the United States.*

He said, "The ideas and the ideals which he [Kennedy] so nobly represented must and will be translated into effective action."

31

A LONG, HEATED DEBATE

On February 10, 1964, the House of Representatives passed the Civil Rights Act by a vote of 290-130. But the bill faced a difficult battle in the Senate. One of President Johnson's longtime friends, Senator Richard B. Russell, a Democrat from Georgia, promised to fight the bill. "We will resist to

President Johnson (left) and Senator Richard Russell didn't agree on the issue of civil rights.

the bitter end any measure or any movement which would have a tendency to bring about social equality," Russell told his fellow senators.

The Civil Rights Act of 1964 threatened many people's way of life. When slavery was legal before the Civil War, blacks were enslaved by white plantation owners and had no rights. After the war, many Americans felt blacks and whites should live separately. They believed each state should decide if segregation was legal. To them, the federal government was interfering by trying to pass the first Civil Rights Act.

Russell organized 18 Southern Democratic senators in a filibuster to delay voting on the bill. Only cloture, or a vote to end the filibuster, could stop the endless speeches. Two-thirds of the 100 senators had to vote for cloture. The filibuster over the Civil Rights Act dragged on for 83 days.

President Johnson used his political skills to convince enough senators to end the filibuster. On June 17, the Senate voted and passed the Civil Rights Act. Johnson signed the

On July 2, 1964, President Johnson signed the Civil Rights Act, as King (directly behind Johnson) and other civil rights supporters looked on.

bill into law on July 2, 1964. King and other civil rights leaders surrounded the president's desk to witness and celebrate the signing.

THE CIVIL RIGHTS ACT

The Civil Rights Act was now a law of the United States. One part of it stated, "All persons shall be entitled to the full and equal enjoyment of the goods, services, facilities, privileges, advantages, and accommodations of any place of public accommodation … without discrimination or segregation on the ground of race, color, religion, or national origin."

The act defined "place of public accommodation" as any inn, hotel, motel, restaurant, cafeteria, lunch counter, or soda fountain. It included movie houses, theaters, concert halls, and sports arenas. The new act did not include private clubs, however, where the general public had not been allowed in the first place.

In addition, the bill included equal rights for women. A woman could not be denied a job just because she was a female. There was an immediate increase in the number of women and minorities in the workplace. Highly skilled jobs

H. R. 7152

Eighty-eighth Congress of the United States of America

AT THE SECOND SESSION

Begun and held at the City of Washington on Tuesday, the seventh day of January, one thousand nine hundred and sixty-four

An Act

To enforce the constitutional right to vote, to confer jurisdiction upon the district courts of the United States to provide injunctive relief against discrimination in public accommodations, to authorize the Attorney General to institute suits to protect constitutional rights in public facilities and public education, to extend the Commission on Civil Rights, to prevent discrimination in federally assisted programs, to establish a Commission on Equal Employment Opportunity, and for other purposes.

Be it enacted by the Senate and House of Representatives of the United States of America in Congress assembled, That this Act may be cited as the "Civil Rights Act of 1964".

TITLE I—VOTING RIGHTS

SEC. 101. Section 2004 of the Revised Statutes (42 U.S.C. 1971), as amended by section 131 of the Civil Rights Act of 1957 (71 Stat. 637), and as further amended by section 601 of the Civil Rights Act of 1960 (74 Stat. 90), is further amended as follows:

(a) Insert "1" after "(a)" in subsection (a) and add at the end of subsection (a) the following new paragraphs:

"(2) No person acting under color of law shall—

"(A) in determining whether any individual is qualified under State law or laws to vote in any Federal election, apply any standard, practice, or procedure different from the standards, practices, or procedures applied under such law or laws to other individuals within the same county, parish, or similar political subdivision who have been found by State officials to be qualified to vote;

"(B) deny the right of any individual to vote in any Federal election because of an error or omission on any record or paper relating to any application, registration, or other act requisite to voting, if such error or omission is not material in determining whether such individual is qualified under State law to vote in such election; or

"(C) employ any literacy test as a qualification for voting in any Federal election unless (i) such test is administered to each individual and is conducted wholly in writing, and (ii) a certified copy of the test and of the answers given by the individual is furnished to him within twenty-five days of the submission of his request made within the period of time during which records and papers are required to be retained and preserved pursuant to title III of the Civil Rights Act of 1960 (42 U.S.C. 1974–74e; 74 Stat. 88) : *Provided, however,* That the Attorney General may enter into agreements with appropriate State or local authorities that preparation, conduct, and maintenance of such tests in accordance with the provisions of applicable State or local law, including such special provisions as are necessary in the preparation, conduct, and maintenance of such tests for persons who are blind or otherwise physically handicapped, meet the purposes of this subparagraph and constitute compliance therewith.

"(3) For purposes of this subsection—

"(A) the term 'vote' shall have the same meaning as in subsection (e) of this section;

"(B) the phrase 'literacy test' includes any test of the ability to read, write, understand, or interpret any matter."

(b) Insert immediately following the period at the end of the first sentence of subsection (c) the following new sentence: "If in any such proceeding literacy is a relevant fact there shall be a rebuttable

traditionally held by white men suddenly were available to women and minorities.

The new law also ensured that people could vote. It said that a person of voting age with a sixth-grade education was considered literate, or able to read, and could vote. In 1965, Congress passed an even stronger law, the Voting Rights Act. It specifically ensured black voters the same rights as white voters.

The Department of Justice now could sue anyone who didn't protect the new rights of blacks. But just a few months after the law was passed, some Southern business owners filed their own lawsuits. They questioned whether the Civil Rights Act was legal under the U.S. Constitution. In one case, *Heart of Atlanta Motel v. The United States*, the U.S. Supreme Court ruled that the Civil Rights Act was legal. It stated that Congress had the power to integrate public places such as hotels, motels, restaurants, stores, and schools.

Now African-Americans could go to places they had

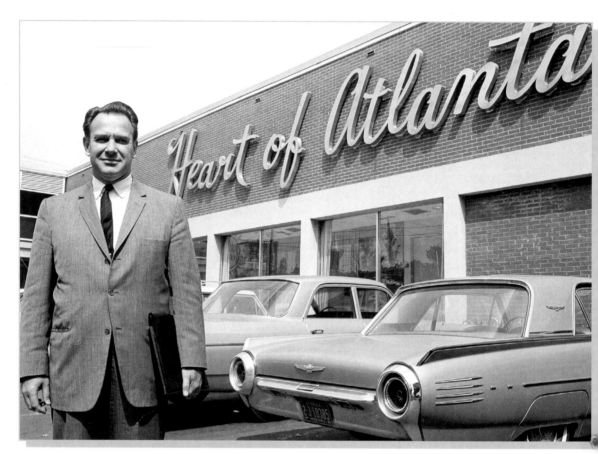

*Morton Rolleston, owner of the Heart of Atlanta Motel, challenged the
Civil Rights Act of 1964 by suing the United States of America.*

never been before. They could shop in stores they had never
visited and sleep in hotels that never before would have
given them a room. Congress threatened to cut off federal
money to any state or local government that didn't obey the
new Civil Rights Act.

A BETTER WORLD

The Civil Rights Act of 1964 guaranteed equal rights and instantly gave people of all races and religions new freedoms. But blacks were still far from equal. Bitter racism remained, and in some places, violence grew among blacks and whites alike.

Riots erupted on college campuses and in cities across the country. In August 1964, three young civil rights workers were killed in Mississippi. On April 4, 1968, a gunman assassinated Martin Luther King Jr. on a hotel balcony in Memphis, Tennessee.

James Earl Ray was later caught and pleaded guilty to the killing. King, one of the greatest civil rights leaders of the era, was dead, but his beliefs and his words lived on. King's principles of equality remind people today that freedom and equality are possible. His words still remind people that blacks and whites and all races deserve the same civil rights.

Police and ambulance workers carried the body of Martin Luther King Jr. from the Lorraine Motel in Memphis, Tennessee, on April 4, 1968.

Although the United States has come a long way in abolishing segregation, the struggle for civil rights still goes on. But one day, perhaps King's hope will come true. The dream he shared at the 1963 civil rights march in Washington, D.C., still lives on in the hearts of many:

40

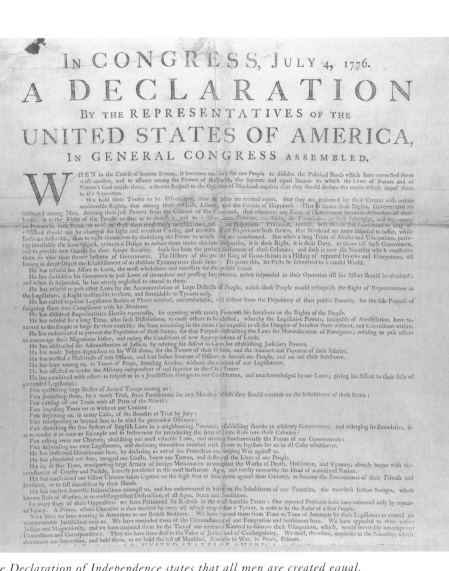

The Declaration of Independence states that all men are created equal.

"I have a dream that one day this nation will rise up and live out the true meaning of its creed: 'We hold these truths to be self-evident, that all men are created equal.'"

GLOSSARY

amendment—formal change made to a law or legal document such as the Constitution.

discrimination—treating people unfairly because of their race, religion, sex, or age

entitled—having the right to do or have something

federal marshals—law enforcement officers for the federal government

gender—designation of male or female

integration—bringing different groups in society together as equals

racism—the belief that one race is better than others

segregation—the separation of groups of people based on their race

42

DID YOU KNOW?

- The civil rights movement began in the 1700s when black slaves in Virginia and white Quakers in Pennsylvania protested the harsh treatment of slaves. Most Americans believe the civil rights movement began with a 1954 Supreme Court decision, *Brown v. Board of Education*. The court ruled that public schools could not separate blacks from whites.

- Some protests are called sit-ins. In 1960, four students in Greensboro, North Carolina, walked into a Woolworth's department store and sat down at a "whites-only" lunch counter. Although they were violating a Jim Crow law, they refused to move until they were served.

- In 1870, the 15th Amendment to the U.S. Constitution gave black men the right to vote. But in 1962, only 5 percent of African-Americans in Mississippi were registered to vote.

43

IMPORTANT DATES

Timeline

1954	On May 17, the U.S. Supreme Court's decision in *Brown v. Board of Education* integrates public schools.
1955	On December 1, Rosa Parks refuses to give up her seat on a bus to a white man and is jailed in Montgomery, Alabama; blacks boycott city buses for more than a year.
1963	On August 28, more than 250,000 protesters march in Washington, D.C., to encourage passage of the Civil Rights Act.
1963	On November 22, President John F. Kennedy is assassinated in Dallas, Texas.
1964	On July 2, President Lyndon B. Johnson signs the Civil Rights Act into law.
1968	On April 4, Martin Luther King Jr. is assassinated on a motel balcony in Memphis, Tennessee.

IMPORTANT PEOPLE

LYNDON B. JOHNSON (1908–1973)

Vice president under John F. Kennedy who became president when Kennedy was assassinated on November 22, 1963; he took his oath of office aboard Air Force One, *the presidential airplane, in Dallas, Texas, and served as president during most of the Vietnam War*

JOHN F. KENNEDY (1917–1963)

President of the United States who introduced what later became the Civil Rights Act but never lived to see it become law; assassinated on November 22, 1963; elected at age 43, he was the youngest man ever elected president and the youngest to die in office

MARTIN LUTHER KING JR. (1929–1968)

Leader of the American civil rights movement who was awarded the Nobel Peace Prize before he was assassinated on April 4, 1968; President Jimmy Carter awarded him the Presidential Medal of Freedom in 1977

ROSA PARKS (1913–2005)

Seamstress whose arrest on a bus in Montgomery, Alabama, prompted blacks to boycott city buses for more than a year; she came to be called the Mother of the Modern Day Civil Rights Movement

WANT TO KNOW MORE?

At the Library

McWhorter, Diane. *A Dream of Freedom: The Civil Rights Movement from 1954 to 1968.* New York: Scholastic, 2004.

Meltzer, Milton. *There Comes A Time: The Struggle for Civil Rights.* New York: Random House, 2001.

Supples, Kevin. *Speaking Out: The Civil Rights Movement, 1950–1964.* Washington, D.C.: National Geographic, 2006.

Treanor, Nick (Ed.). *The Civil Rights Movement.* San Diego: Greenhaven Press, 2003.

On the Web

For more information on this topic, use FactHound.

1. Go to *www.facthound.com*

2. Type in this book ID: 0756524598

3. Click on the *Fetch It* button.

FactHound will find the best Web sites for you.

On the Road

National Civil Rights Museum

450 Mulberry St.

Memphis, TN 38103

901/521-9699

A museum in the motel where

Martin Luther King Jr. was

assassinated

Birmingham Civil Rights Institute

520 16th St. N.

Birmingham, AL 35203

866/328-9696

A center for education and

discussion about civil rights

Look for more We the People books about this era:

The 19th Amendment

The Berlin Airlift

The Dust Bowl

Ellis Island

The Great Depression

The Korean War

Navajo Code Talkers

Pearl Harbor

The Persian Gulf War

The San Francisco Earthquake of 1906

September 11

The Sinking of the U.S.S. Indianapolis

The Statue of Liberty

The Titanic

The Tuskegee Airmen

The Vietnam Veterans Memorial

A complete list of We the People titles is available on our Web site:
www.compasspointbooks.com

INDEX

About the Author

Jason Skog is a writer who lives in Brooklyn, New York, with his wife and son. He has been a newspaper writer for 11 years, covering education, courts, police, government and youth issues. His work has appeared in magazines and newspapers. This is his third book for young readers.